WALKING CLOSE

the VALE of WHITE HORSE
in Oxfordshire

Number Forty Four in the popular series of walking guides

Contents

Walk		Miles	Page No
1	Faringdon Folly	$5^{3}/_{4}$	4
2	Uffington Wood	6	6
3	Frogmore Brook	8	8
4	Buckland Warren	6	10
5	Wayland's Smithy	$5^{3}/_{4}$	12
6	Whitehorse Hill	11	14
7	Segbury Camp	4	17
8	Cornhill Lane	$4^{1}/_{2}$	18
9	Lyde Copse	5	20
10	Buscot Weir	5	22
11	Badbury Clump	6	23
12	Woolstone Down	$5^{1}/_{2}$	25
13	Odstone Combes	$4^{1}/_{4}$	27

Walked, Written and Drawn by Clive Brown
© Clive Brown 2008 – 2013

Published by Clive Brown
ISBN 978-1-907669-44-6

PLEASE
Take care of the countryside
Your leisure is someone's livelihood

Close gates
Start no fires
Keep away from livestock and animals
Do not stray from marked paths
Take litter home
Do not damage walls, hedgerows or fences
Cross only at stiles or gates
Protect plants, trees and wildlife
Keep dogs on leads
Respect crops, machinery and rural property
Do not contaminate water

Although not essential we recommend good walking boots; during hot weather take something to drink on the way. All walks can easily be negotiated by an averagely fit person. The routes have been recently walked and surveyed, changes can however occur, please follow any signed diversions. Some paths cross fields which are under cultivation. All distances and times are approximate.

The maps give an accurate portrayal of the area, but scale has however been sacrificed in some cases for the sake of clarity and to fit restrictions of page size.

Walking Close To have taken every care in the research and production of this guide but cannot be held responsible for the safety of anyone using them.

During very wet weather, parts of these walks may become impassable through flooding, check before starting out. Stiles and rights of way can get overgrown during the summer; folding secateurs are a useful addition to a walker's rucksack.

Thanks to Angela for help in production of these booklets

Views or comments?
walkingcloseto@yahoo.co.uk

Reproduced from Ordnance Survey Mapping on behalf of The Controller of Her Majesty's Stationery Office.   © Crown Copyright License No. 100037980.

Walking Close to the Vale of White Horse

The Vale of White Horse stretches from near Swindon to the Thames between Didcot and Abingdon, bordered in the north by a low ridge separating it from the Thames and to the south by the Berkshire Downs. Most of the Vale historically was part of Berkshire, moving to Oxfordshire in 1974. The vale is drained by the River Ock flowing from its source near Little Coxwell into the Thames near Abingdon. The area is known for the white horse cut into the hillside near Uffington, the stylised figure was first identified as a horse by local monks in the 11th century. Recent scientific studies have dated construction to between 1400 and 600BC, making it by far the oldest hill figure in this country. At least 50 other horses and other shapes have been cut from the 18th century onwards; the newest horse was created near Folkestone in Kent in 2003. More than 50 others have been lost due to poor maintenance; the grass soon grows back over the surface if they are not looked after.

The Ridge Way is at least 5000 years old. Running along the high ground it keeps away from the marshy areas that made travelling so difficult and avoids wooded areas likely to shelter thieves and outlaws. The track became a National Trail in 1973, the 87 mile Ridgeway Path goes from Overton Hill near Avebury to Ivinghoe Beacon in Buckinghamshire.

Legends relate that if a traveller on the Ridge Way left a silver coin with his horse overnight in Wayland's Smithy (walks 5 and 6), he would return the next morning to find that his horse had been reshod. Wayland was the blacksmith to the gods in North German mythology brought over with the Saxon invaders and used to describe something they didn't understand and were perhaps a little afraid of. The site is actually a Neolithic barrow or tomb, built around 3700BC as a timber chamber covered in earth. A stone chamber was built on the top of this about 300years later, the remains of this later chamber are what can be seen today.

A statue of the Saxon King Alfred the Great graces the centre of Wantage, the town where he was born in 849.

Kelmscott Manor (walk no 10), was from 1871 the country home of William Morris the designer, writer and artist. He died at the house in 1896 and is buried in the village churchyard.

We feel that it would be difficult to get lost with the instructions and map in this booklet, but recommend carrying an Ordnance Survey map. The walks are on Explorer Map no. 170; Landranger coverage at a smaller scale spreads over three maps nos. 163, 164 and 174. Roads, geographical features and buildings, not on our map but visible from the walk can be easily identified.

1   Faringdon Folly

5¾ Miles   2½ Hours

Park in Faringdon, pay and display; toilets, cafés, shops and other facilities. Start from the Market Place. Will be muddy when wet.

1 Go up towards the church and turn right into Church Street. Keep ahead at the junction and go straight on past the signpost along the narrow potholed road. Go through the gate and carry on up the fenced path, past Church Path Farm and Grove Lodge to the stile level with Haremoor Farm.
2 Step over this stile and cross the field and the stile in the fence opposite. Keep direction, bearing right, over the field away from the fence. This field may be under cultivation but a path should be well marked within any crop. Carry on to the signposted stile ahead.
3 Turn right and follow the grass track through the gate to the road in Littleworth. Continue for 75yds to the signpost and turn right along the enclosed path through the metal gate and up the left hand field edge. Go over the stile in the corner and keep along the left hand field edge up to the A420.
4 Take the narrow roadside path to the left, past the junction and the bus shelter. Cross carefully over this busy road to the signpost and carry on ahead along the double farm track between fields. Continue with the tall hedge to the left; turn left at the end and almost immediate right down to the ruin of Tagdown Barn.
5 Turn right along the track parallel to the trees on the left, go through the wide hedge gap and maintain direction with the hedge to the right. Bear right past the white gate and take a track which should be visible within any crop over the field; keep this line over a farm road and the next section of field and go through the gate. Bear left along the field edge with the fence to the left, back to the A420.
6 Cross carefully, turn left and almost immediate right at the signpost, over the stile. Keep ahead over the field (a path should be well marked) and continue up the slope on the right hand field edge with the trees to the right. Carry on through the trees past the Folly and go down the narrow tarmac path to the road. Turn right down to the junction and left back to the town centre.

The 100ft tower of Faringdon Folly was built in 1935 on the site of a medieval castle and a Civil War fort. It was the last folly of its kind to be built in this country.

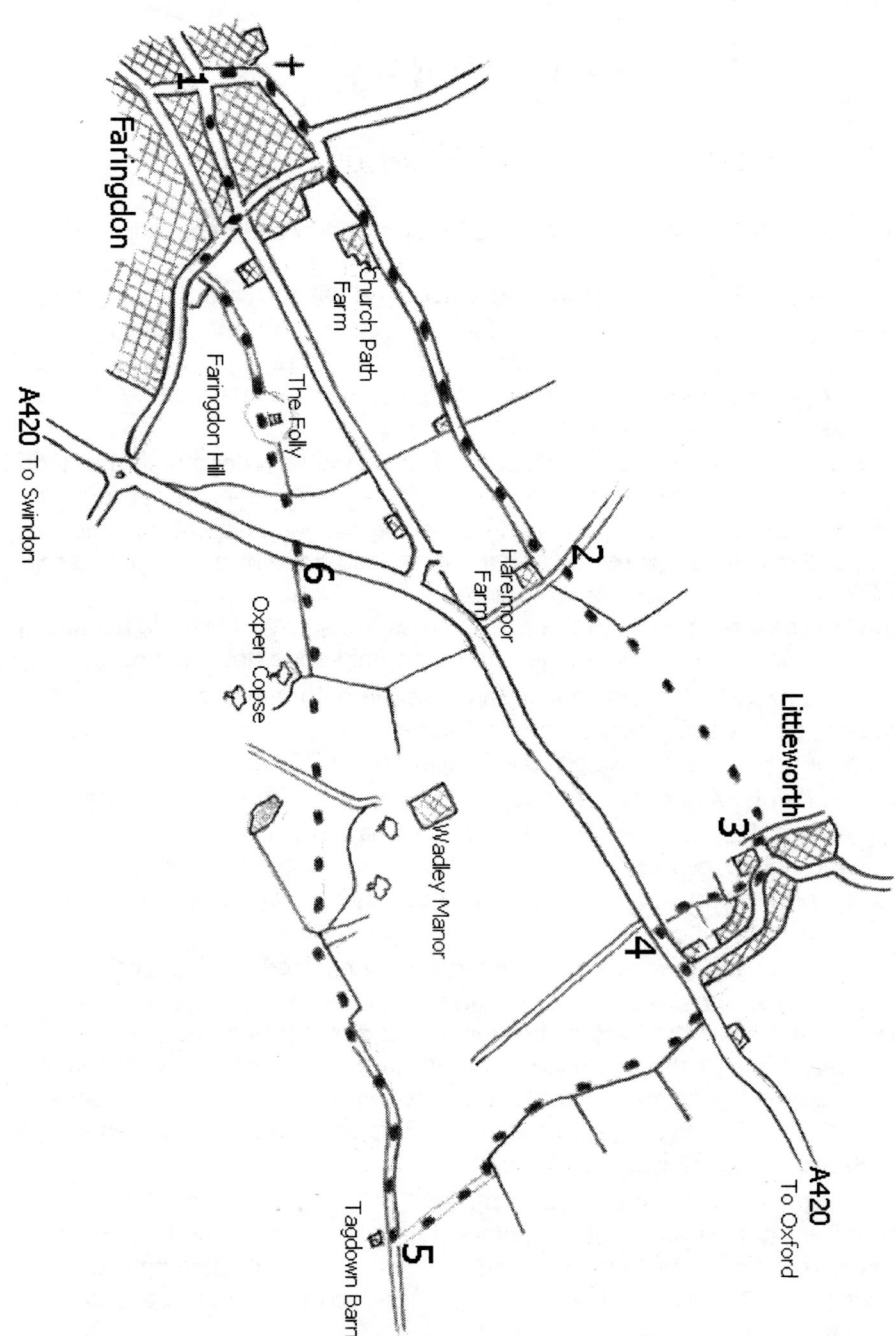

2   Uffington Wood

6 Miles   3 Hours

Use the car park at the village hall in Uffington. Shop and pubs in the village.

1   Start form the village hall; facing away from the hall turn right from the entrance along the roadside path to the footpath signpost on the right. Cross the footbridge, go through the trees and up the left hand edge of the playing field. Exit through the gap by the swings and keep ahead on the grass path between houses. Cross the stile and carry on along the backs of the houses.

2   Bear right over a stile and turn left on the left hand field edge with the hedge to the left, keep direction over a series of stiles. At the hedge ahead bear left across the open field, go over the stile and carry on along the wide grass track between the hedge and the trees. At the end bear left and continue through the trees with the stream to the left. Cross the footbridge and turn right, back to the original direction with the stream now to the right. Cross the stile and turn right, through the wide gap, then turn immediate left along the field edge up to the road.

3   Turn left for 85yds to the signpost and take the path uphill, go through the gate and turn right up the stiff slope of the field edge with Uffington Wood to the right. Keep direction on less severe slopes all the way to the Ridgeway Path.

4   Take the hardcore path left for two thirds of a mile to the next signpost on the left and go down the hardcore farm track to the road. Cross and continue ahead on the right hand field edge with the hedge to the right. At the bottom step over the stile and carry on ahead with the hedge still right through two gates; bear right along the track to the road.

5   Turn left down the roadside path through Fawler village, past the first signpost at the derestriction signs to the second signpost as the road swings left. Turn right over the stile and cross the field in the signposted direction, this field may be under cultivation but the path should be well marked within any crop. Go over the stile, through the gap in the trees and across the footbridge. Bear left over the field, a track should be visible, to the far corner. Turn left and follow the field edge with Stutfield Brook to the right, up to the road.

6   Go along the road to the left, up to the end of Uffington Gorse. Turn right over the stile at the signpost and take the signposted direction over the field to the opposite corner. Cross the farm road and the next field to the stile near the far corner, keep direction through the trees and over two more stiles to the road. Turn left and bear left to the main road at the village hall.

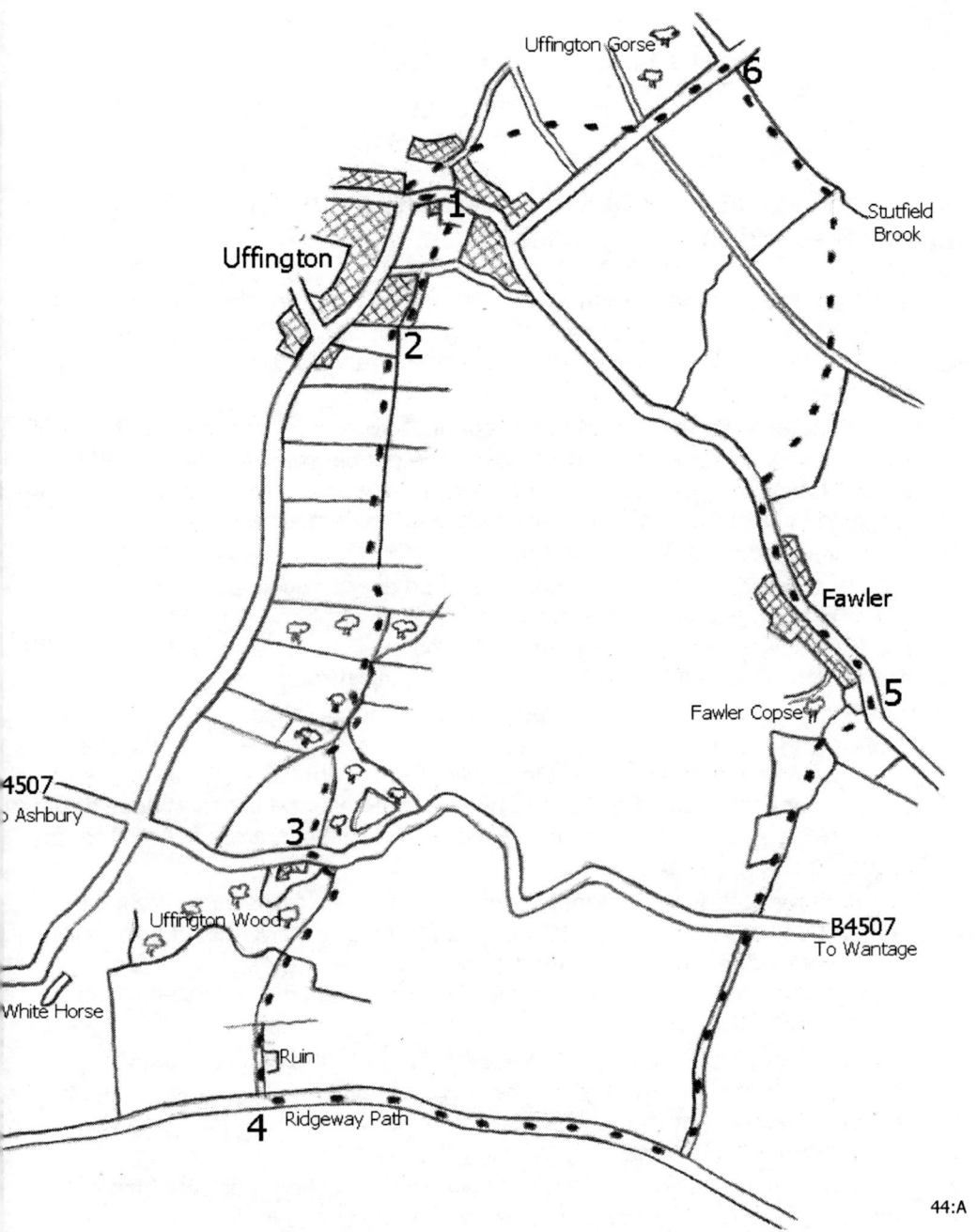

3   Frogmore Brook

8 Miles   4 Hours

Find a parking space in Stanton in the Vale, no toilets; small supermarket and shop/post office. Several pubs.

1   Start from the junction of High Street with the A417. Turn right, up to the 'Horse and Jockey' and take the footpath on the right hand side signposted to Shellingford. Go right of the gateposts, keeping the fence and the hedge to the left and cross over the stile ahead.
2   Bear slight left over the next stile and continue with the fence to the left. Step over the next stile and bear slight right across the double stile/footbridge in the hedge gap. Carry on ahead over thus field which may be under cultivation although a path should be well marked within any crop over the almost hidden stile/footbridge. Bear right across the field and take the farm track to the left.
3   Cross the footbridge/stile in the corner and go over the field at a slight angle to the right. On the other side of the farm road take a right hand diagonal over the field and the midway fence, through the gate and over the footbridge in the opposite corner. Bear right and almost immediate left through the gate.
4   Turn right and go through the wide gateway, continue ahead left of the barns on to the concrete farm road. Turn right, up to the barn, turn left and take the driveway right up to the village street in Shellingford. Turn left past the church to the footpath signpost, cross the stile and go over the field and the footbridge at the bottom right. Carry on through the bushes, over the stile and cross the field to the kissing gate at the top by the road.
5   Turn right for 30yds to the signpost and take the wide grass path through the metal gate. Continue ahead, slight left, across the field (a track should be visible) go over the footbridge and through the kissing gate. Keep ahead, over the next field, through the boundary and the next field; at the final boundary bear left to Wickwood Farm.
6   Bear right with the fence to the left and turn right at the corner along the gravel drive for 40yds. Turn right through the narrow gate, cross the fence at the marker disc and continue ahead with the hedge to the right. Go through the hedge gap 40yds left of the corner and carry on through the trees.
7   Take a right hand diagonal across the field (the path should be well marked), after 300yds turn right at an unmarked crossroads, up to the hedge corner. Maintain direction along the farm road with the fence to the right, follow this track left and keep ahead up the slope all the way to the A417.
Completed on Page Ten.

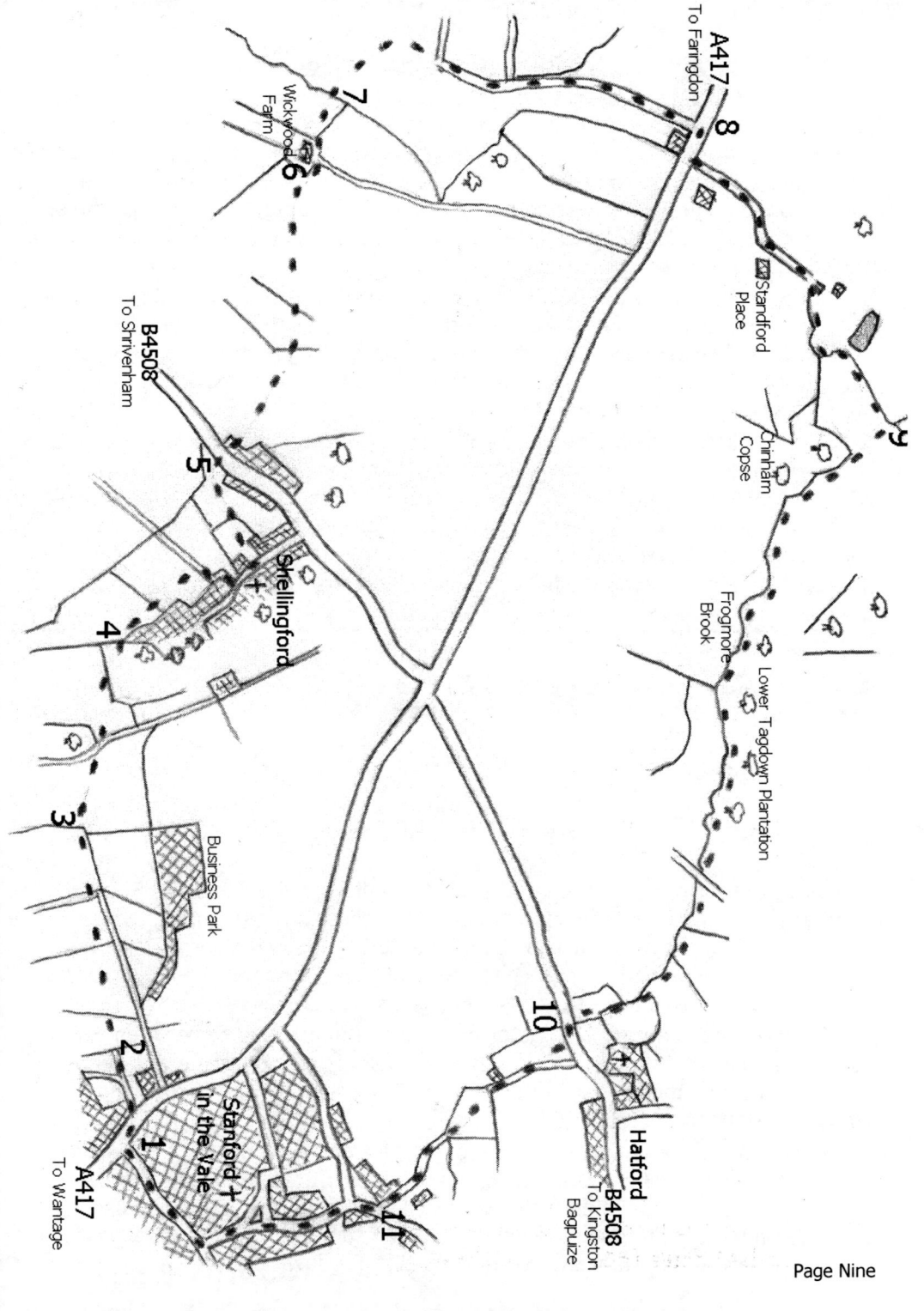

Completion of 3 Frogmore Brook from the previous Page

8 Turn right along the wide grass verge for 120yds, cross carefully and go through the stone gateway at the footpath signpost. Keep ahead past Standford Place and carry on with the wall to the right, to the metal gate; turn right through the narrow metal gate and bear left between the trees and the fence. Bear further left between posts and turn right, across the corner of the field and along the path past the end of the hidden small lake. Keep ahead between fields with the barbed wire fence to the left.

9 At the corner of the trees turn right and follow the track left of Chinham Copse, carry on with Frogmore Brook and the trees to the right. Cross the entrance road to the quarry and keep ahead trees still to the right, bearing right through an open gate. Turn right, through a metal gate and left with the brook now left, carry on over the stile and on to the B4508.

10 Turn left across the bridge and right over the stile at the signpost, step over the stile two thirds of the way along on the left. Continue along the track to the right with the fence to the right, past Little Hatford, between hedges and over the stile next to the gate. Bear left over the stile on the left and take the path right between barbed wire fences, over the footbridge. Keep on the path ahead to the road.

11 Carry on ahead, along Chapel Road and follow the road right at the end, back to the starting point at the junction with the A417.

4   Buckland Warren

6 Miles   3 Hours

Use the car park in Buckland village, pub the 'Lamb Inn', no other facilities.

1 Leave the car park entrance to the left and follow Orchard Road to Buckland Road at the T-junction. Turn left and walk up to the footpath signpost hidden in the wall gap on the right as the houses end. Bear left at the end, over the stile and continue with the barbed wire fence to the right. Step over the stile, bear left past the house to the A420 and cross this busy road very carefully.

2 Carry on ahead through the gates along the tarmac driveway between trees. Follow the road left and right, around Home Farm past the dovecote and keep ahead on the now muddy hardcore surface. Go through the metal gate and bear left on the track to the crossroads.

3 Turn right, follow the wide track through the trees and bushes of Buckland Warren, keep ahead at a crossroads on a wide grassy track. Carry on through the golf course, between the metal railings; bear left through the hedge gap and continue on the path through the field. Continue straight on at the road, as it swings left take the track ahead down to derelict Tagdown Barn.

4 Take the path to the right between fields, up a slight slope; turn left and right, on the right hand field edge up to the A420. Cross with care and turn right along the roadside path to the junction.

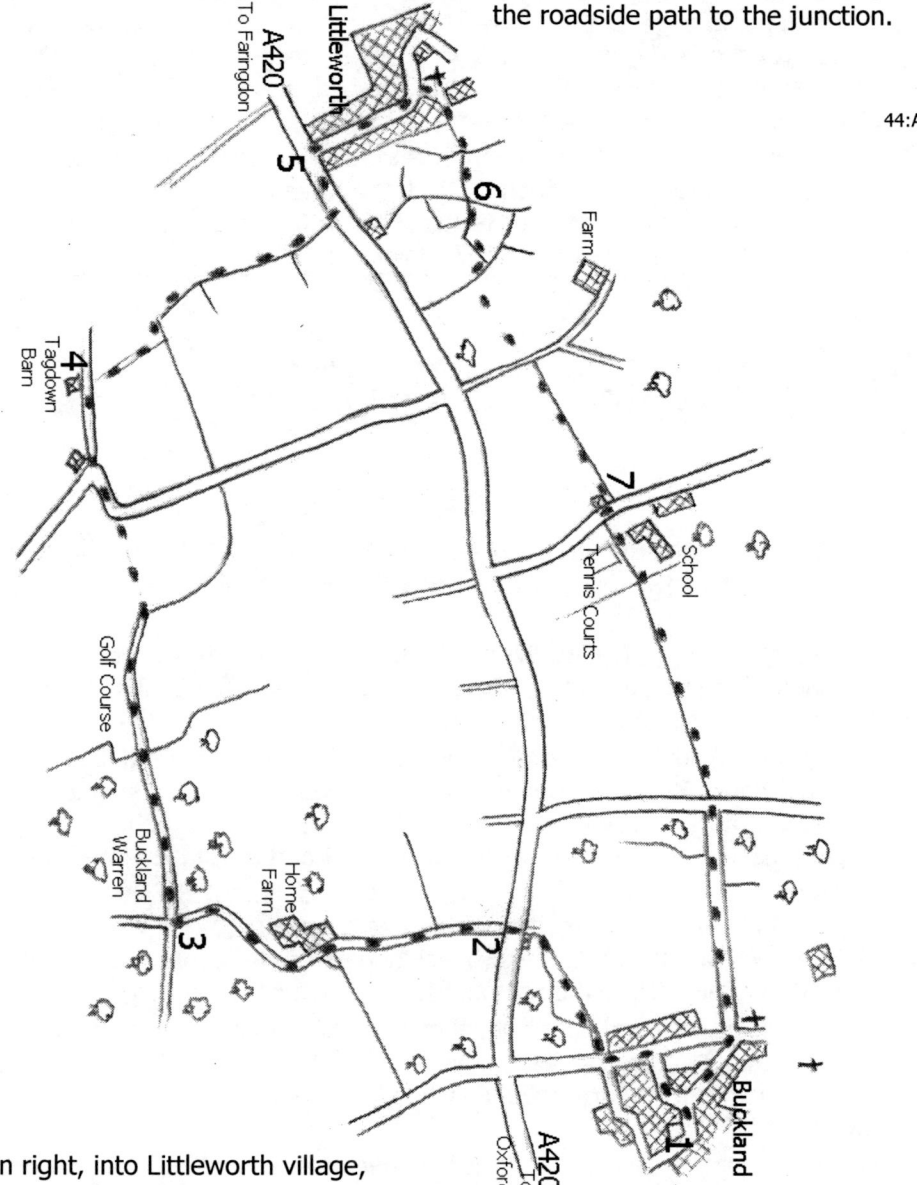

5 Turn right, into Littleworth village, follow the road left and turn right at the church. Turn further right with the fence to the right and take the path between the fence and the trees. Keep direction; bear right through barriers and a gate, downslope between fences and step over the stiles and footbridge at the bottom.
Completed on the next Page (Twelve).

Completion of 4 Buckland Warren from the previous Page

6   Continue uphill between the posts, over the stile at the top and bear right on the left hand field edge to the double stile on the left. Cross these stiles and continue over the field (a track should be visible); keep direction across the driveway and the left hand field edge with the hedge to the left. At the end carry on along the fenced path past the house to the road.

7   Turn right for 120yds to the signpost and take the path left, between the school and the tennis courts. Keep ahead through the trees and follow the wide path on the field edge ahead with the trees to the right, to the road at a T-junction. Take the road ahead back into Buckland to find your vehicle.

5   Wayland's Smithy

$5^3/_4$ Miles $2^1/_2$ Hours

Use the small parking space at Ashbury Folly, where the Ridgeway Path crosses the B4000, south east of Ashbury village. No facilities.

1   Take the Ridgeway Trail to the south west for 400yds to the four way signpost and turn left along the field edge with the hedge to the left. Continue between fields, passing right of the clump of trees.

2   Step over the stile at the corner of Hailey Wood and carry on ahead with the fence to the right. Keep direction with Middle Wood now left, cross the stile next to the mounds of Alfred's Castle and bear right with the trees to the left. Go over the next stile; take the path left with the trees still left and down the slope with Ashdown house and Park to the left.

3   In the dip bear left and keep ahead on the tarmac road past Ashdown Farm. Cross back over the B4000 and take the signposted route uphill, along the track right of the summit. (Note the reason it is called Weathercock Hill).

4   Step over the stile and bear right across the field which may be under cultivation although a path should be well marked to the flagpole on the opposite side. Take the hardcore farm road left/ahead downslope to the crossroads at the byway signpost.

5   Turn left along the wide grass track between fences and keep on this track alongside the narrow belts of trees all the way to the Ridgeway Path.

6   Turn left along this substantial track, past Wayland's Smithy, back to the car park and your vehicle.

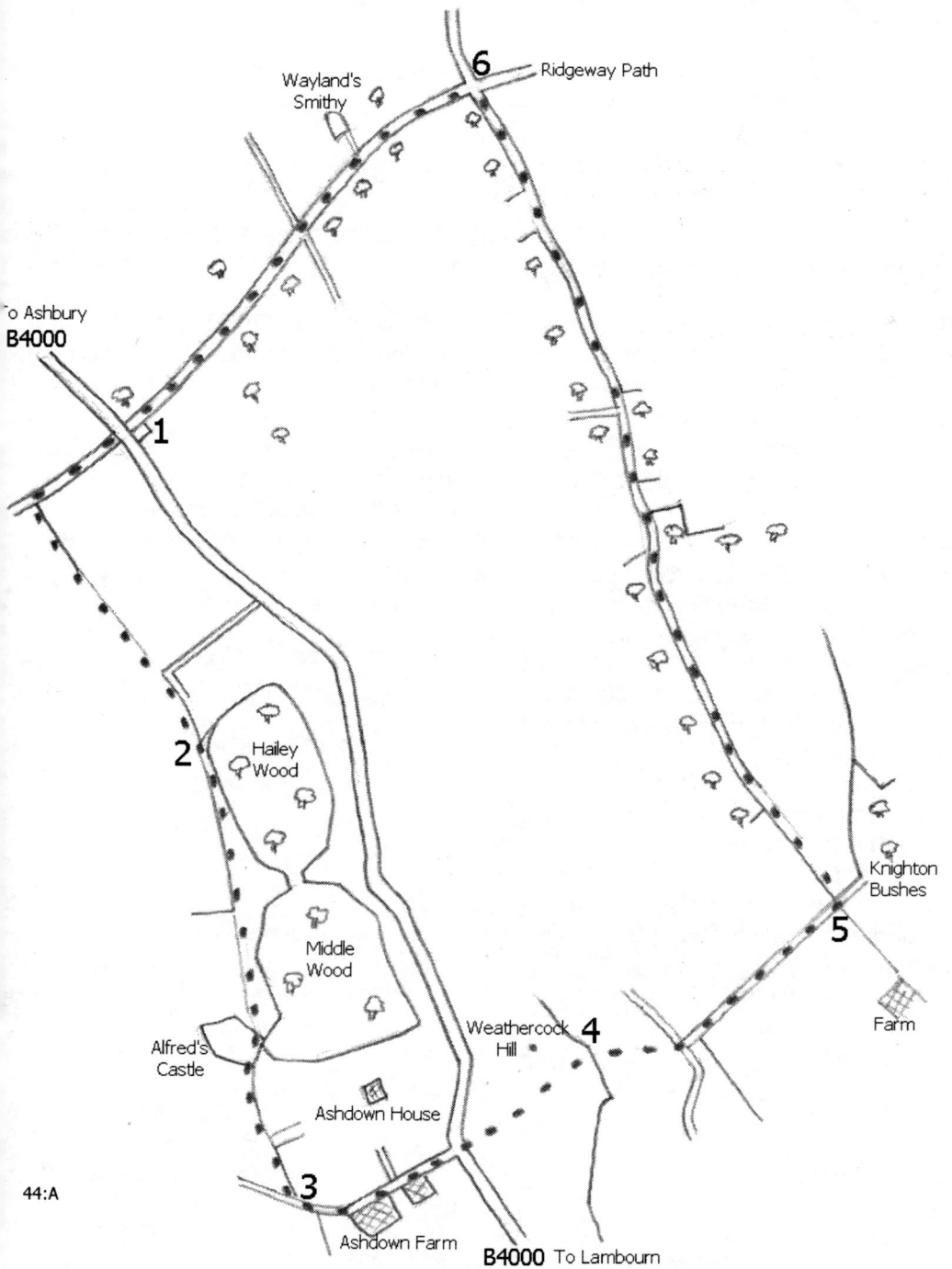

6 Whitehorse Hill

11 Miles   5¼ Hours

Use the car park at the village hall in Uffington. Shop and pubs in the village. The route can be very muddy in winter.

1 Go out of the car park entrance and turn left along Broad Street, at the footpath signpost turn right into Waylands. Exit at the far left, between houses and cross the stile; continue up the left hand field edge over the footbridge and on to the road.

2 Cross and go into the driveway opposite, bear left then right past the front of the thatched cottage. Cross the dyke and bear left over the field which may be under cultivation although a path should be well marked within any crop. Carry on across the farm road and bear left through the marked gap, over the footbridge and on to the road.

3 Step over the stile opposite and bear slight right over the next footbridge; keep ahead on the path through the trees. At the road go through the gate and turn right across the footbridge and along the path with the stream to the right. Continue over the stile/footbridge along the right hand field edge, bearing left to the right hand corner. Cross this footbridge and carry on along the path parallel to but 30yds from the left hand field edge, up to the road.

4 Keep ahead on the left hand field edge, with the hedge to the left, all the way to the footbridge; bear left across the field (a track should be well marked) through the gates at the end and step over the stile. Bear left to the stile right of the farm and continue slight left to the far corner, over the farm road and stiles to the stile at the '30' signs.

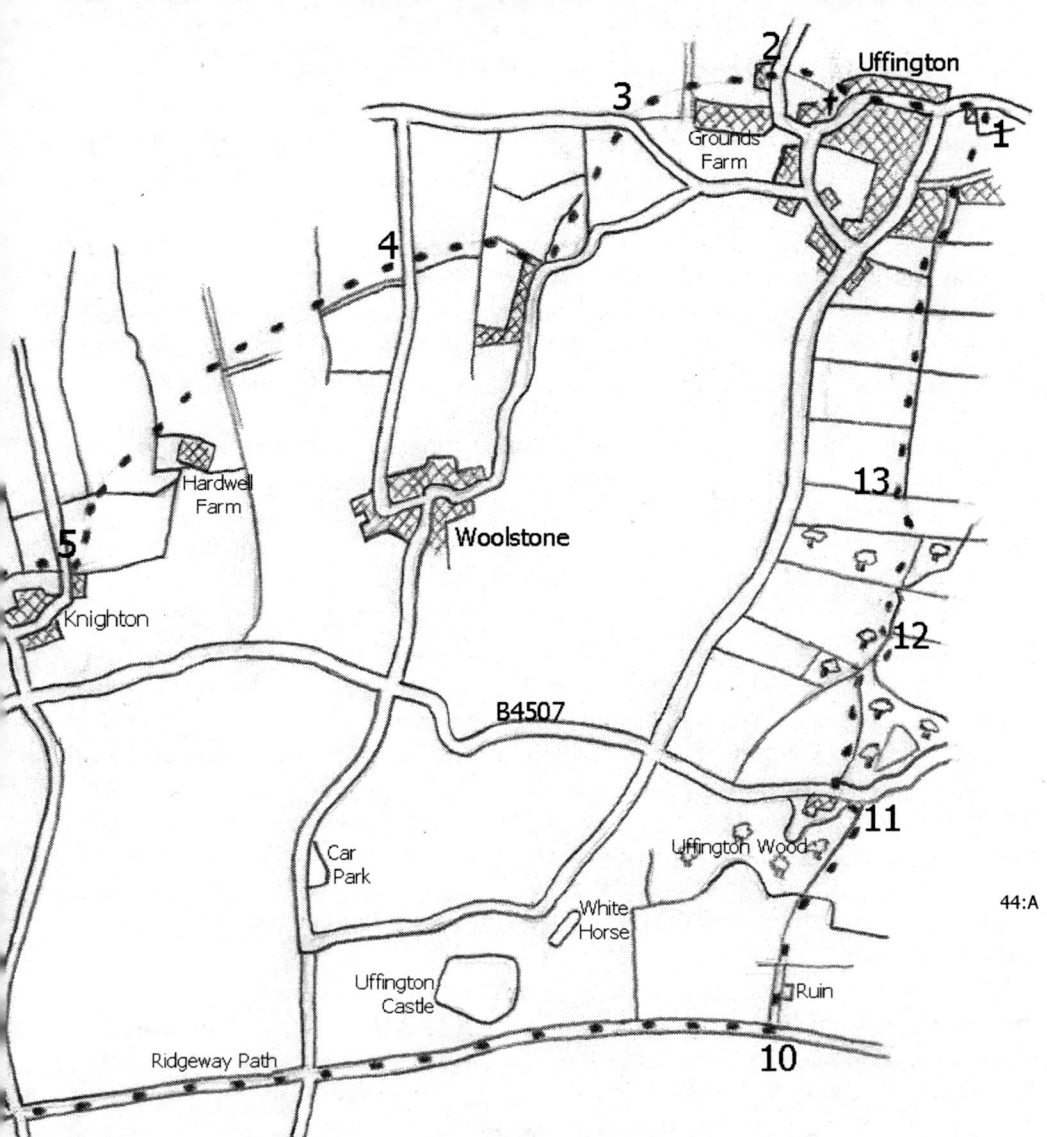

5 Cross the road and keep ahead along the left hand field edge, over the stile and bear left upslope out of the gate at the top left. Bear right on the road and keep straight on, past the signpost, through the brick gateposts and left of the clock, (Compton House is off to the left) to the church. Continue through the black kissing gate and follow the field edge with the fence to the left through the gate at the marker disc. Bear right upslope through the narrow gate and bear further right over the field (a track should be visible) through the wide gap ahead. Keep direction with the hedge to the left to Odstone Farm.
Completed on the next Page (Sixteen)

Completion of 6 Whitehorse Hill from the centre Pages

6 Bear right (the path should be visible) and keep direction through the dip with the pond to the right. Continue direction with the hedge now left, parallel to the power lines, all the way to the end corner and take the path left, down to the road at Kingstone Winslow.

7 Turn left and immediate right on the tarmac road downhill, bear right past the mill and keep ahead up the narrower path to the road at Ashbury. Continue ahead up Chapel Lane, straight on at the end past the footpath signpost between stone houses; step over the stile and carry on up the path between the hedge and the fence. Cross the next stile and bear right on the right hand field edge across the stile at the end.

8 Take the farm road left, cross the road and carry on uphill with the houses to the left up to the boundary. Turn right, with the hedge to the right along the field edge to the marker post; turn left on a path which should be well marked running uphill parallel to but 30yds away from the treeline on the right. Carry on to the substantial Ridgeway path at the top of the slope.

9 Follow this path for just over three miles, past Wayland's Smithy, several junctions and over Whitehorse Hill with Uffington Castle hill fort to the left.

10 At the next signpost turn left on a track between fields, past the ruins of some small farm buildings; cross the stile and bear right, through the kissing gate. Carry on downhill with Uffington Wood to the left and exit through the kissing gate at the bottom left, down the track to the road.

11 Turn left for 130yds to the signpost, turn right and follow the right hand field edge with the hedge to the right. Cross the stream in the bottom right hand corner and continue direction with the hedge now left to the stile/footbridge in the next corner. Carry on along the left hand field edge, past a marker post to the next marker post near the corner.

12 Turn left over the sleeper footbridge and right, back to the original direction, through the trees with the stream now right. Go past the footbridge and keep ahead with the trees still right; cross the double stile, bear left and step over the next stile in the hedge.

13 Continue ahead along the right hand field edge, *(look out for the memorial at ground level, for the crew of a World War II Wellington bomber).* At the stile at the end, bear right and follow the path left between the fence and the hedge. Keep direction between houses over the gravel drive and the sports field to the car park and your vehicle.

The church at Uffington, often referred to as the 'Cathedral of the Vale', was built in the 13th century. The unusual design incorporates a central octagonal tower; the tower once supported a tall spire which fell down during a storm in 1740.

7 Segbury Camp

4 Miles   2 Hours

Find a parking space in Letcombe Regis, there is often space in the car park at the playing field on Bassett Road.

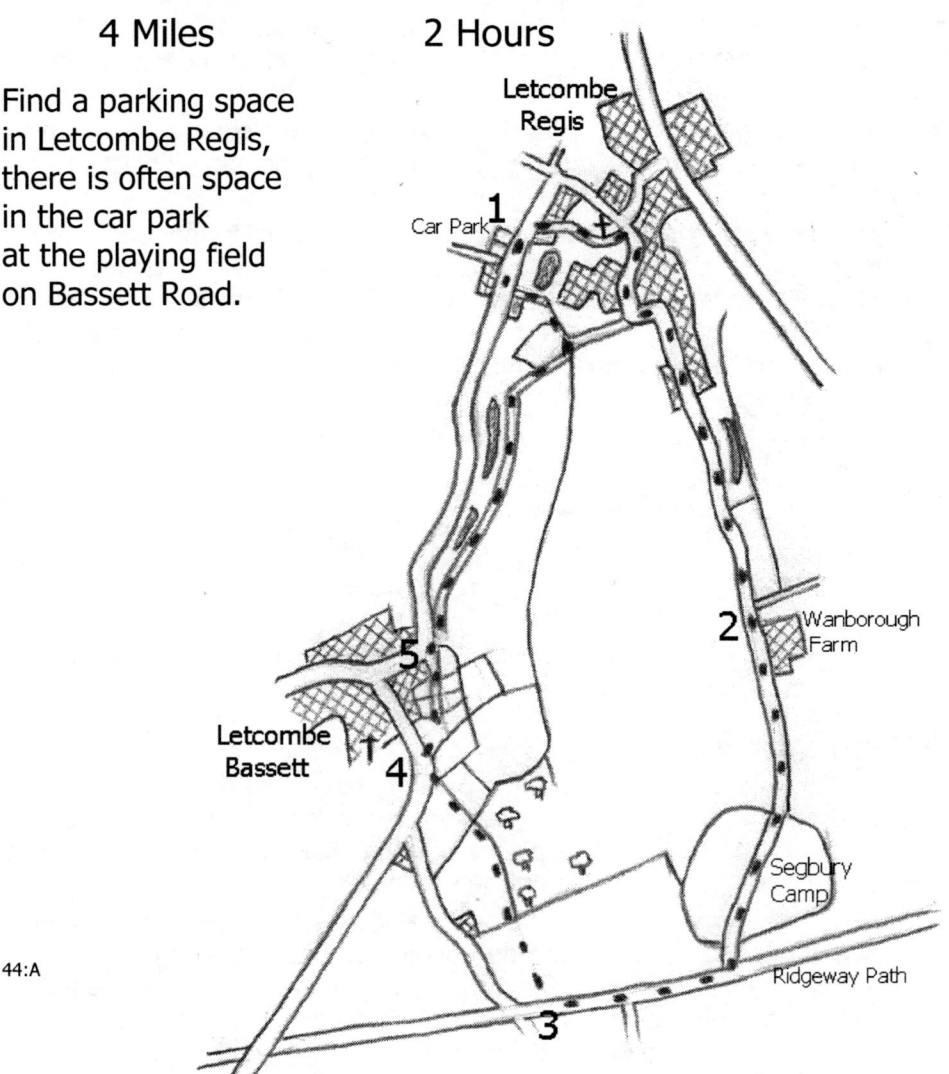

1   At the car park entrance turn left down the road to the thatched cottage. Turn right along the footpath, between the ivy covered fence and the chain link fencing, passing right of the church to the junction. Turn right signposted 'Village Downs Only' and follow the road upslope out of the village.

Completion of 7 Segbury Camp from the previous Page

2   Go past Warborough Farm, further uphill and through the ramparts of Segbury Camp Iron Age hill fort to the Ridgeway Path. Turn right, to the signpost for Letcombe Bassett and step over the stile on the right.

3   Take the track downslope through the grass; keep direction further downhill over the stiles and through the dip to the stile at the top right. Go over and follow the left hand field edge to the road.

4   Turn right down to the signpost and climb the track up the steep bank. Turn right and bear left over the grass and cross the stile at the end of the brick wall. Take the path left, over the stile down nearly to the road.

5   Turn right at the signpost along the path above and parallel to the road with the fence to the right. Keep ahead along this enclosed path to the narrow gate and bear right, still between fences. Bear left at the end for 90yds and step over the stile on the left at the signpost. Go down the right hand field edge with the trees to the right; go through the corner and the gate, cross the footbridge to the road and turn right back to the village to find your vehicle.

---

8   Cornhill Lane

$4^{1}/_{2}$ Miles   2 Hours

Use the car park for the playing field, at the end of Childrey Way in East Challow. No toilets, but all other facilities in the village. Muddy in wet weather.

1   Turn right from the car park entrance up to the crossroads and take the bridleway Cornhill Lane to the right, down to the footbridge over the course of the disused Wilts and Berks Canal. Cross and turn left along the old towpath to the road at the edge of West Challow. Keep ahead through the gate to the tarmac farm road and turn left over the bridge with wooden railings.

2   Bear right on this tarmac track, up the gentle slope between the fence and the hedge all the way to Childrey. Keep ahead through the houses, bearing right to the main street at the Chapel. Turn, past the duck pond and bear left just before the post office down to the T-junction; turn left and continue ahead slight right upslope on the narrower tarmac track between the barbed wire fence and the hedge.

3   At the marker disc on the fence post turn right, still uphill between hedges. Cross the road and carry on parallel to the telegraph poles, bearing left down to the bottom left corner. Turn right at the footpath signpost and take the field edge left, with the hedge to the left, step over the stile in the corner and continue along the enclosed path to the road in Letcombe Regis.

4 Turn left and walk down to the corner; take this byway to the left and follow it left and right up to the T-junction of tracks. Turn right, along this track all the way to the road and turn left up to the T-junction. Cross and keep direction, back along Cornhill Lane down to the crossroads of tracks; turn right back to the car park and your vehicle.

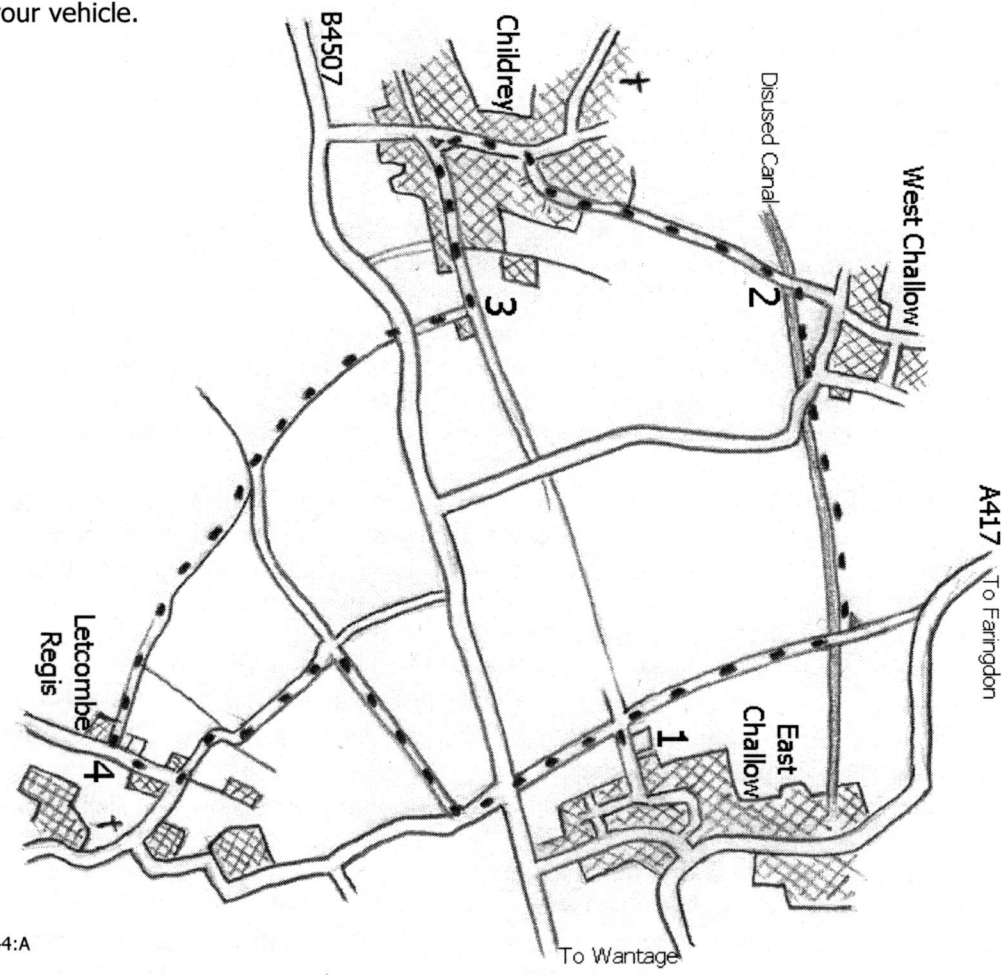

44:A

The disused waterway is the course of the Wilts and Berks Canal. Linking the River Thames at Abingdon with the Kennet and Avon Canal at Semington near Trowbridge, the canal was completed in 1810. Never very successful, its busiest period had been transporting materials to build the Great Western Railway on an almost parallel route. The railway then of course took a great deal of the canal's business. In 1901 a major part of the aqueduct at Stanley near Chippenham collapsed and the rest of the canal was gradually run down, closing in 1914.

9 Lyde Copse

5 Miles   2½ Hours

Find a parking space in Baulking village; there is sometimes room near the church; no facilities. The walk can be very muddy and is not very well signposted or waymarked.

1 Start from the church, turn left over the cattle grid further into the village; carry on along the road with the common to the left. As the road swings left at the end, keep ahead slight right past the signpost to the far corner.

2 Go through the wide gap and bear left over the field, which may be under cultivation but a track should be visible within any crop, to a hedge gap and go through the green gate. Keep direction across this field and go through the gate at the bottom right, turn right, go through the wide metal gate and bear left to the line of trees.

3 Very carefully, cross this broken ramshackle footbridge and bear right on the left hand field edge with the hedge to the left and bear slight left. Go through the gate and continue with the hedge still left up a slight slope, through the double gate with its double fastening. Keep ahead over a farm road, through double gates in a hedge and bear right (a track should be visible), to the road.

4 Cross and carry on between electric fences, continue over the farm bridge between dykes and slight left over the next field through which a path should be well marked. Go through the gap and take the path left at the fork (the track again should be visible) up the sloping field.

5 At the top, turn left on the wide grass track between fields; continue slight right with the trees of Lyde Copse to the right. Turn right in the corner through the gate and immediate left. Keep the original direction through the trees with the barbed wire fence to the right to the unmarked junction at the top of a descent.

6 Turn left, with a barbed wire fence still right, bear left with this track between the fence and the trees, past South Farm House and up the tarmac drive. After 220yds turn right through the gate in the narrow hedge gap, bear left to the far left corner through the gate to the road.

7 Cross and keep ahead, over the field and go through the gate on the right, turn immediate left along the hedged bridleway, Long Lane. Continue on the track on the right hand field edge with the hedge to the right; at the bottom carry on past the signpost over the field parallel to the hedge on the left. Go through the marshy area, over the footbridge and through the gate. Carry on through the gate right of the thatched cottage, to the road.

44:A

8 Turn left for 300yds to the stile in the narrow hedge gap, step over and walk past the stables to the boundary and cross the footbridge. Follow the left hand field edge into the corner and turn right within this same field with the hedge still left, through the boundary and up the slope, through the gate at the top.

44:A

9 Turn immediate left through the wide blue gate and up the right hand field edge with the hedge to the right. Go through the blue (left hand) gate of the furthest two gates on the right. Cross the field and go through the wide, dark green gate ahead. Follow the wide track to the right, back into Baulking and turn right along the narrow path back to the church.

10   Buscot Weir

5 Miles   2¼ Hours

Use the National Trust car park in Buscot village, toilets, small shop and café adjacent.

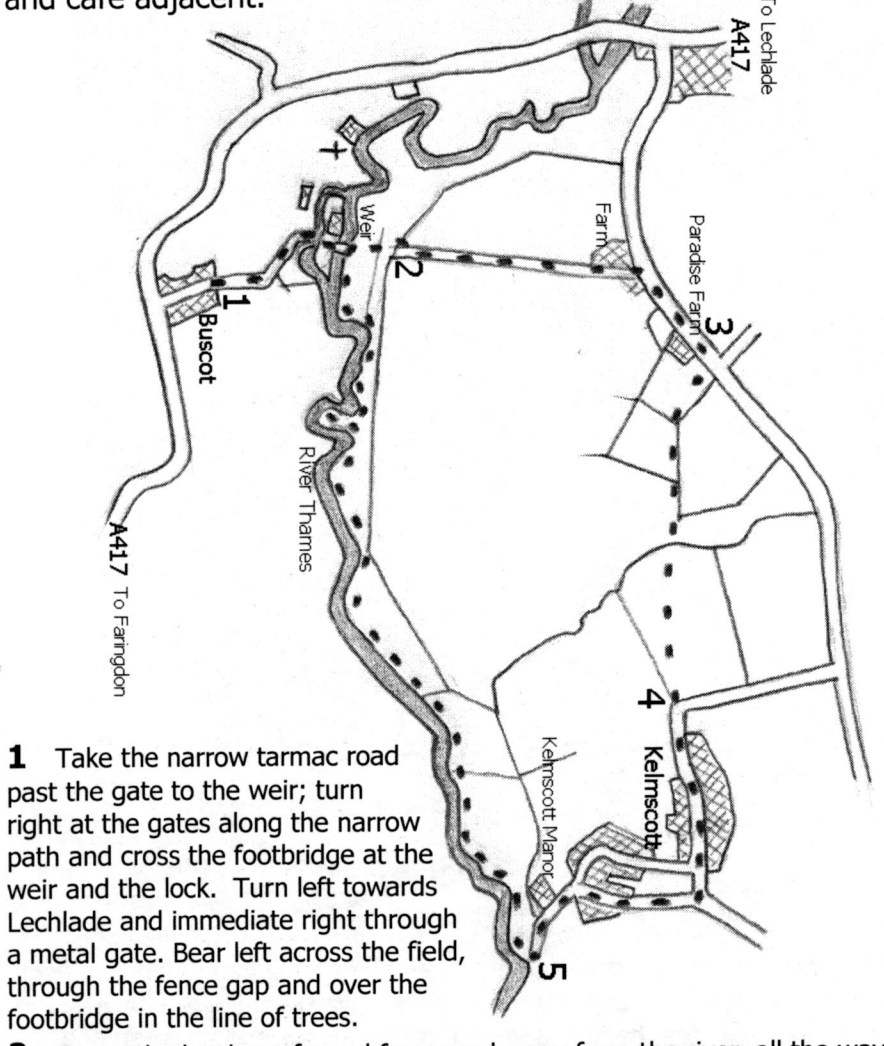

1   Take the narrow tarmac road past the gate to the weir; turn right at the gates along the narrow path and cross the footbridge at the weir and the lock. Turn left towards Lechlade and immediate right through a metal gate. Bear left across the field, through the fence gap and over the footbridge in the line of trees.

2   Go up the hardcore fenced farm road away from the river, all the way to the farm and the road. Turn right along the road to the second signpost on the right, past Paradise Farm.

3 Step over the stile and cross the field and the stile in the bottom corner. Carry on along the left hand field edge of this and the next field, keep ahead over the field which may be under cultivation although a path should be well marked to the road at a corner.
4 Continue ahead along the road into Kelmscott to the end at a T-junction and turn right down to the bottom. Bear left towards the manor and further right at the signpost, down to the Thames Path.
5 Turn right and follow the path along the riverbank back to Buscot Weir, the car park and your vehicle.

11   Badbury Clump

6 Miles   3 Hours

Use the car park at Badbury Hill on the B4019 west of Faringdon, no facilities.

1 Go through the gate at the back of the car park and turn left, follow the wide path downhill with the ramparts to the right. Bear right, keep straight on down the slope and carry on along the narrower track to the bottom of the slope.
2 Maintain direction out of the trees up the field edge with the trees to the right. Turn left at the boundary for 25yds and cross the footbridge to the right. Keep ahead along the right hand field edge; go through the double gates and over the concrete road.
3 Bear left up the hardcore farm track through the gate and along the track; take a left hand diagonal across the field which may be under cultivation although a path should be well marked. Step over the footbridge/stile, cross the corner of the field and the next stile; follow the path ahead between the fence and the hedge to the footbridge in the bottom of the dip.
4 Keep ahead through the trees of Fern Copse and maintain direction up the slope of the right hand field edges to the road. Cross, continue ahead over the stile opposite on the track into the field and turn left down the field edge. Go through the kissing gate, down the village street, past the church into Coleshill and over the B4019. Keep straight on between the walls and pass through the green gate and the metal gate.
5 Bear left across Coleshill Park and keep direction over three stiles, carry on left over the hill to the corner of the trees. Turn left along the farm track with Flamborough Wood to the left and continue with Ashen Copse on the right. Cross the tarmac farm road and keep ahead left of Ashen Copse Farm along the left hand
The map and completion of text are on the next Page (Twenty Four)

Completion of 11 Badbury Clump from the previous Page.

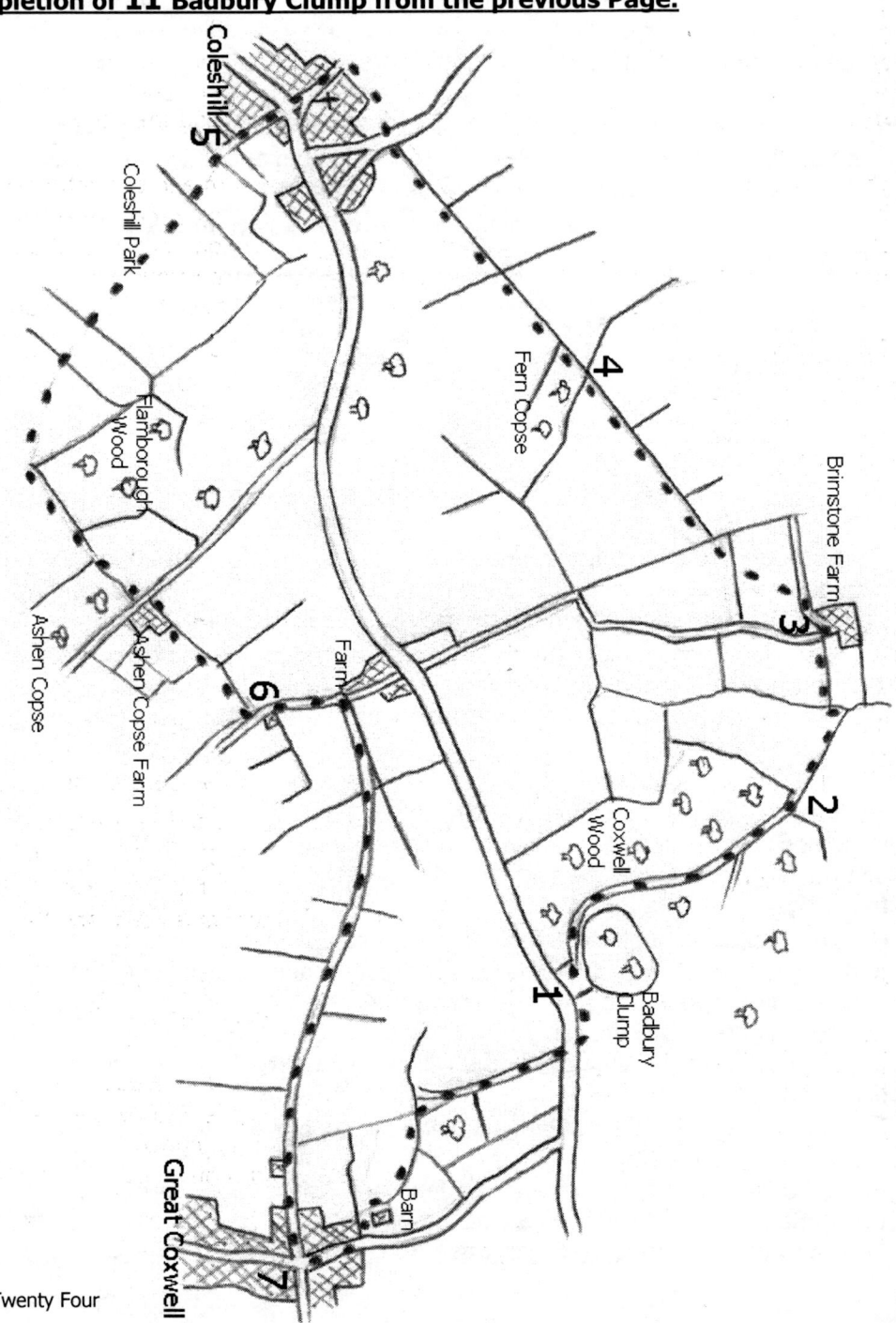

Page Twenty Four

field edge with the fence and hedge to the left. Carry on along the next field edge to the corner and go through the gate.

6 Turn left past the house, up the hardcore farm road, bear right and turn right, through the metal gate; continue ahead between the fence and the hedge all the way into Great Coxwell village.

7 Take the main street left to the signpost at the tithe barn and turn left past the barn, through the hedge gap. Turn right and follow the hedge, bearing left to the stile/footbridge; step over and go through the trees. Carry on uphill with the trees to the right and keep ahead between fences to the road. Go through the gateway opposite and follow the path along the left hand field edge back to the car park and your vehicle.

---

12   Woolstone Down

$5^1/_2$ Miles $2^1/_2$ Hours

Use the car park at White Horse Hill, no facilities.

1 Go out of the entrance and turn left uphill along the road; keep ahead on the hardcore/potholed surface over the Ridge Way. Continue downslope past the barns and carry on along the field edge and the wide path, through the first belt of trees all the way down to the far corner to the far corner of Knighton Bushes Plantation.

2 Turn left with the trees to the left, down to the signpost and bear left uphill between fields to the signpost at the top and turn left through the fence gap.

3 Go up the wide grass track along Woolstone Down, with the trees to the left and the low white posts to the right, bearing left past the marker post and keep ahead between white posts.

4 Pass through the gateway at the right hand end of the trees and follow the path through the dip. Turn left for 50yds and take the path right, between fields further up the hill, back to the Ridge Way.

5 Turn right for 90yds, go through the gate on the left and walk past the Ordnance Survey marker around the edge of Uffington Castle. Follow the track away from the ramparts, past the marker post and down the narrow hardcore path. Cross Dragonhill Road and take the path on a left hand diagonal back to the car park and your vehicle.

The Map is on the next Page (Twenty Six)
44:A

12 Woolstone Down Map

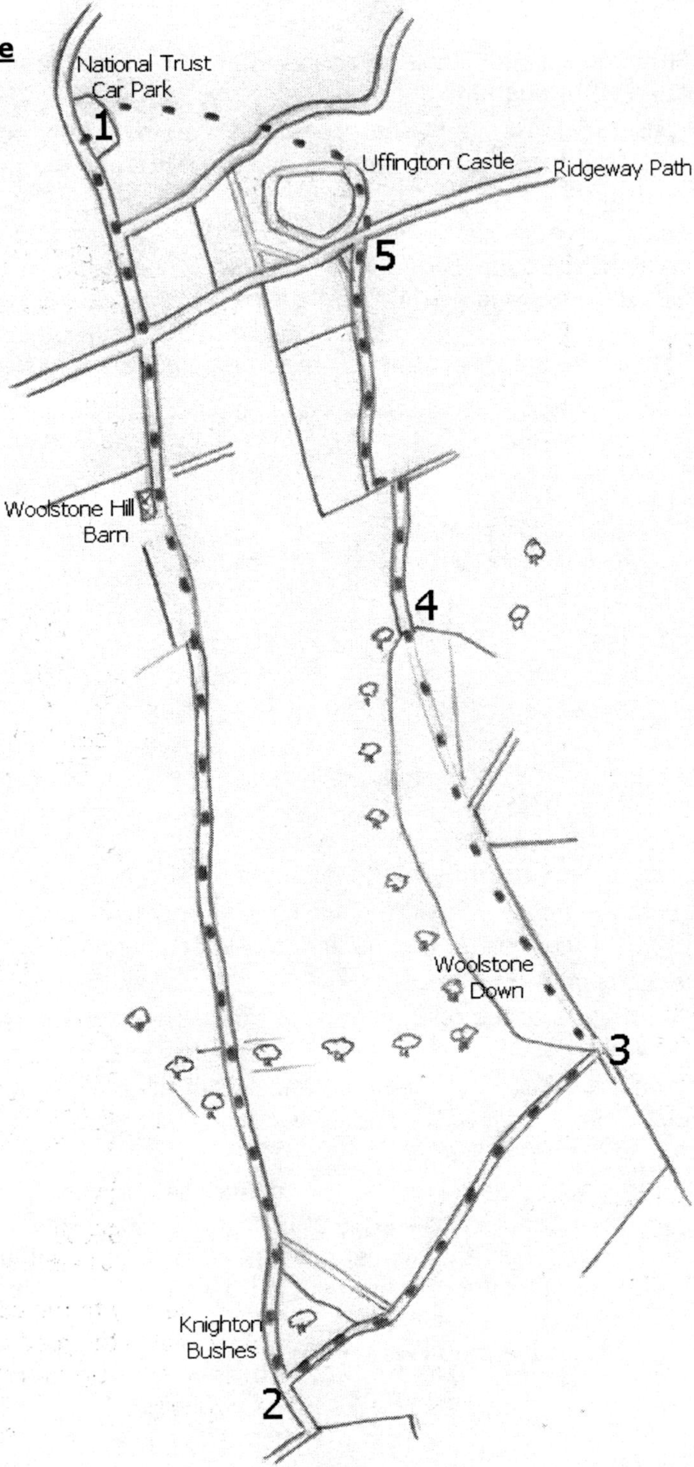

National Trust Car Park
1

Uffington Castle
Ridgeway Path
5

Woolstone Hill Barn

4

Woolstone Down

3

Knighton Bushes
2

Page Twenty Six

44:A

13 Odstone Combes

4¼ Miles   2 Hours

Find a parking space in Ashbury village. No toilets; pub the 'Rose and Crown', small post office/shop.

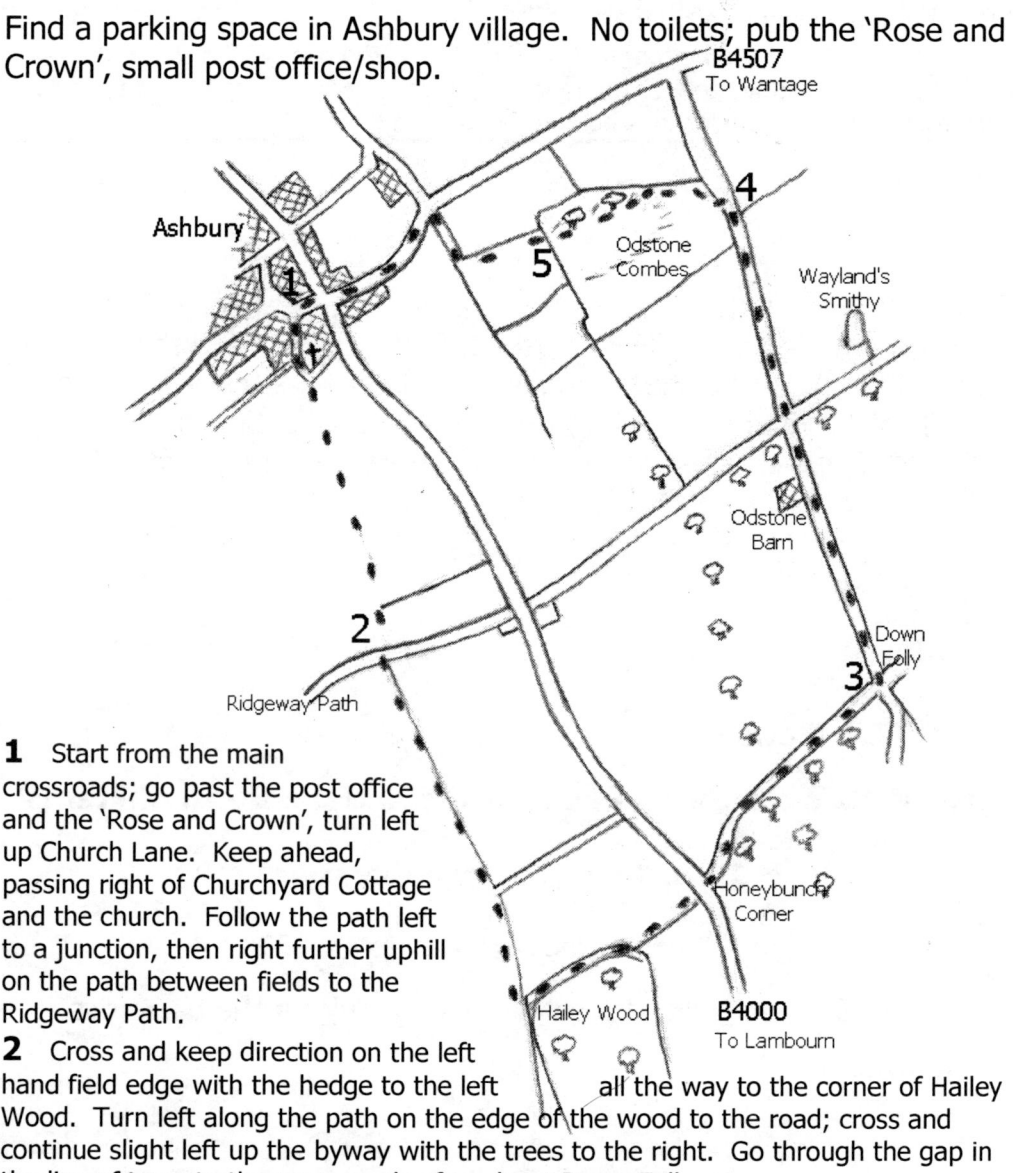

1 Start from the main crossroads; go past the post office and the 'Rose and Crown', turn left up Church Lane. Keep ahead, passing right of Churchyard Cottage and the church. Follow the path left to a junction, then right further uphill on the path between fields to the Ridgeway Path.

2 Cross and keep direction on the left hand field edge with the hedge to the left all the way to the corner of Hailey Wood. Turn left along the path on the edge of the wood to the road; cross and continue slight left up the byway with the trees to the right. Go through the gap in the line of trees to the cross roads of tracks at Down Folly.

Completion of 13 Odstone Combes from the previous Page

3 Take the wide path to the left past Odstone Barn back to the Ridgeway Path. (Wayland's Smithy is 300yds to the right). Keep direction straight on.

4 About 30yds after the concrete track starts downhill, turn left at an unmarked point on a narrow track through a gully to a stile marked by a disc. Step over and bear right then left along the right hand side of Odstone Combes with the fence to the right, descending through the trees.

5 Cross the stile at the bottom and continue along the base of the slope with the field to the left, bearing right to the road. Turn left carefully along the side of this busy road to the crossroads in Ashbury and your vehicle.

Other 'Walking Close to' guides are available for locations in Essex, Suffolk, Cambridgeshire, Hertfordshire, Bedfordshire, Berkshire, Devon, Dorset, Buckinghamshire, Northamptonshire, Leicestershire, Norfolk, Nottinghamshire, Lincolnshire, Oxfordshire, Somerset, Wiltshire, Warwickshire, Worcestershire, Herefordshire, Hampshire and the Southern Lake District.

Also by Clive Brown:-

'Easy Walking in South Bedfordshire and the North Chilterns'

37 Walks in your favourite style

Published by the Book Castle @ £8-99

e-mail Clive on walkingcloseto@yahoo.co.uk for the best price